FACES
ARE
THE
MIRROR
OF
THE
SOUL

Welcome to the world of digital portraits by
Paola Minekov

Minekov is an artist who creates expressive and captivating images with a distinctive style of hand-drawn line art

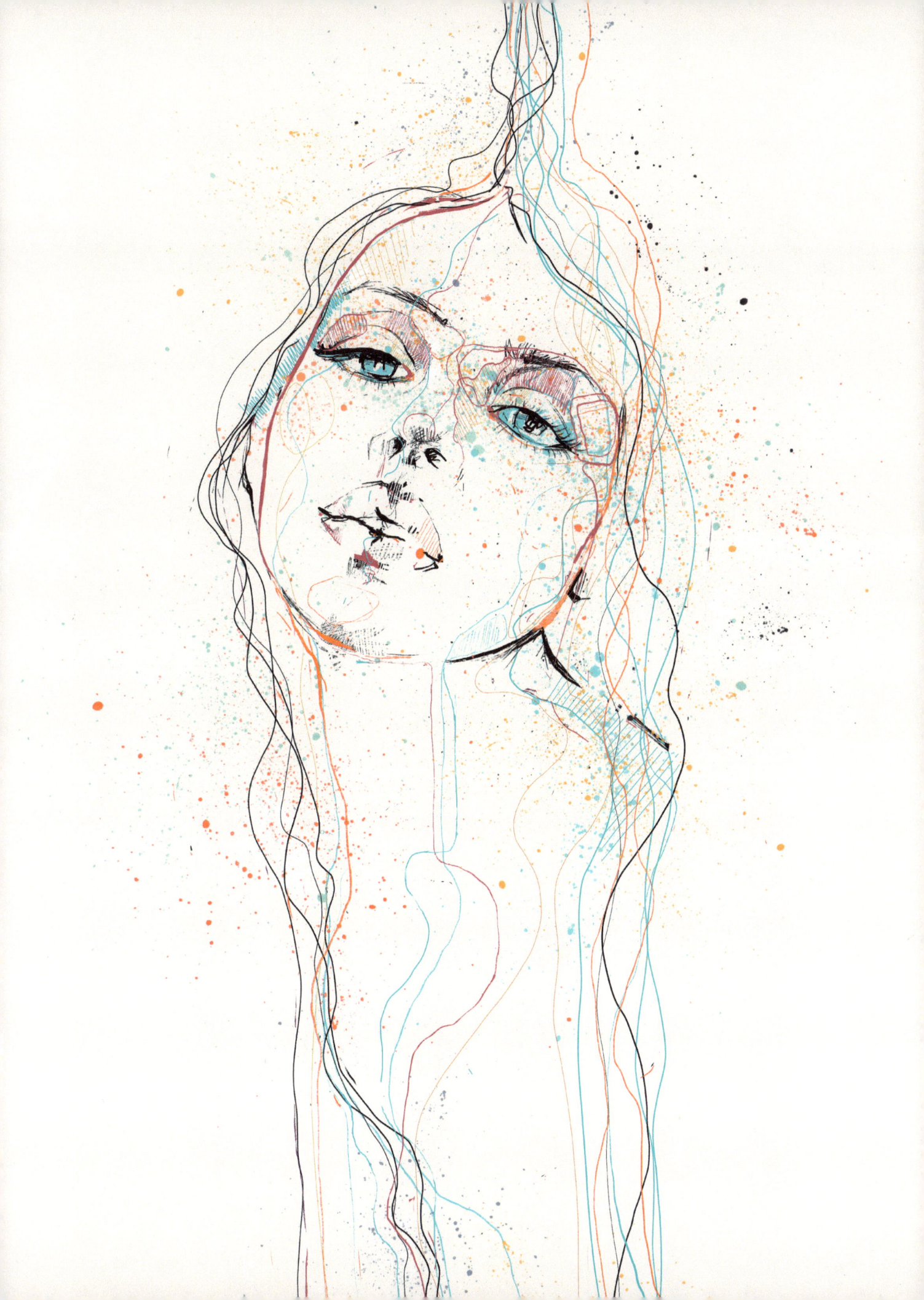

# The Portrait Commission Process

Paola's portrait commissions process is designed to ensure that you receive a professional, high-quality artwork you can cherish for years to come.

The process begins with an initial online consultation to discuss your vision for the artwork.

The majority of Paola's digital portraits are based on reference photos. In the initial consultation Paola will provide a list of the reference images needed to create the portrait. Once the your photos are gathered, Paola will begin sketching and creating the portrait.

Paola always provides regular progress updates during the creation of your portrait.

Once your portrait is complete, Paola will review the artwork togehter with you to ensure your complete satisfaction.

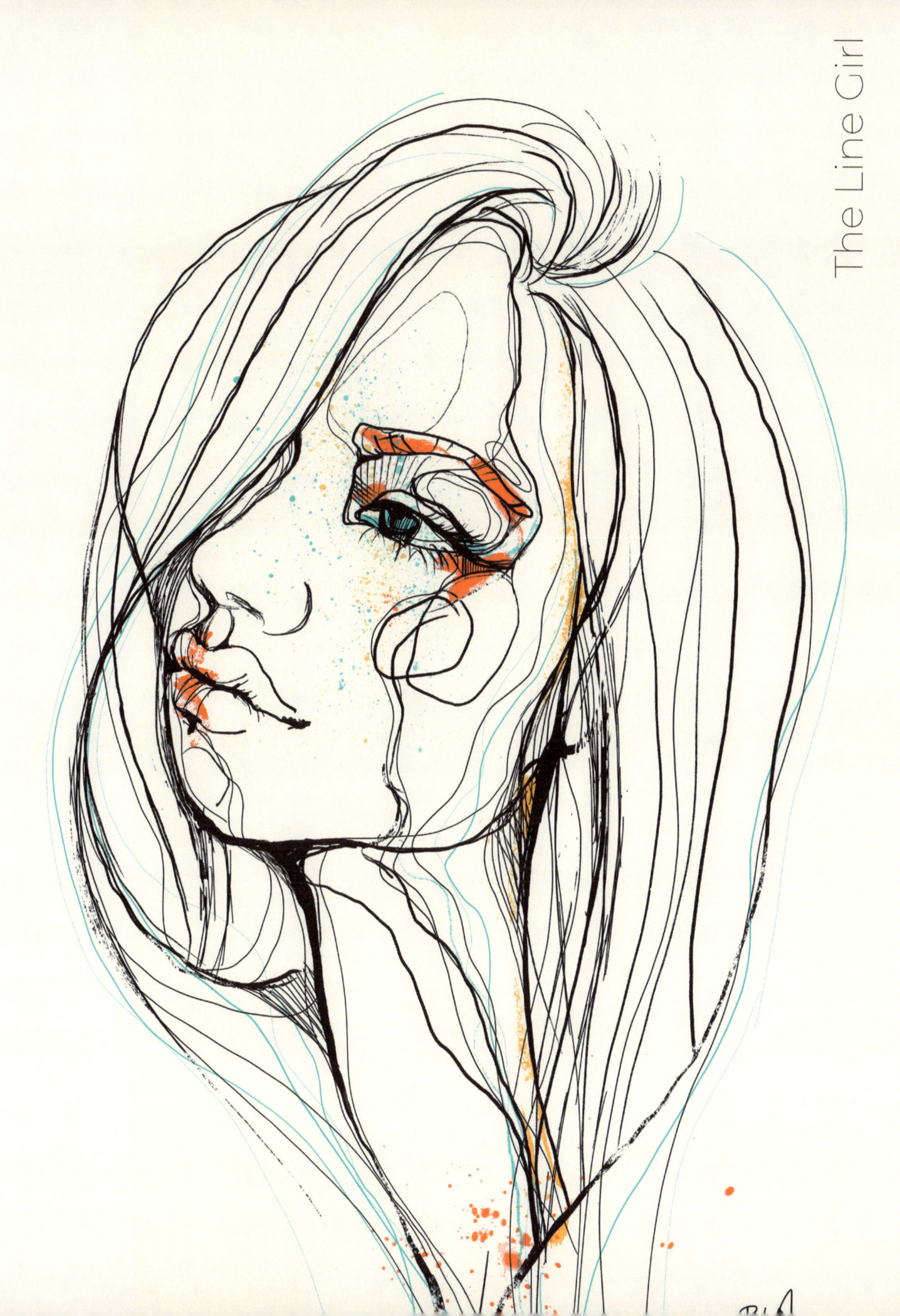

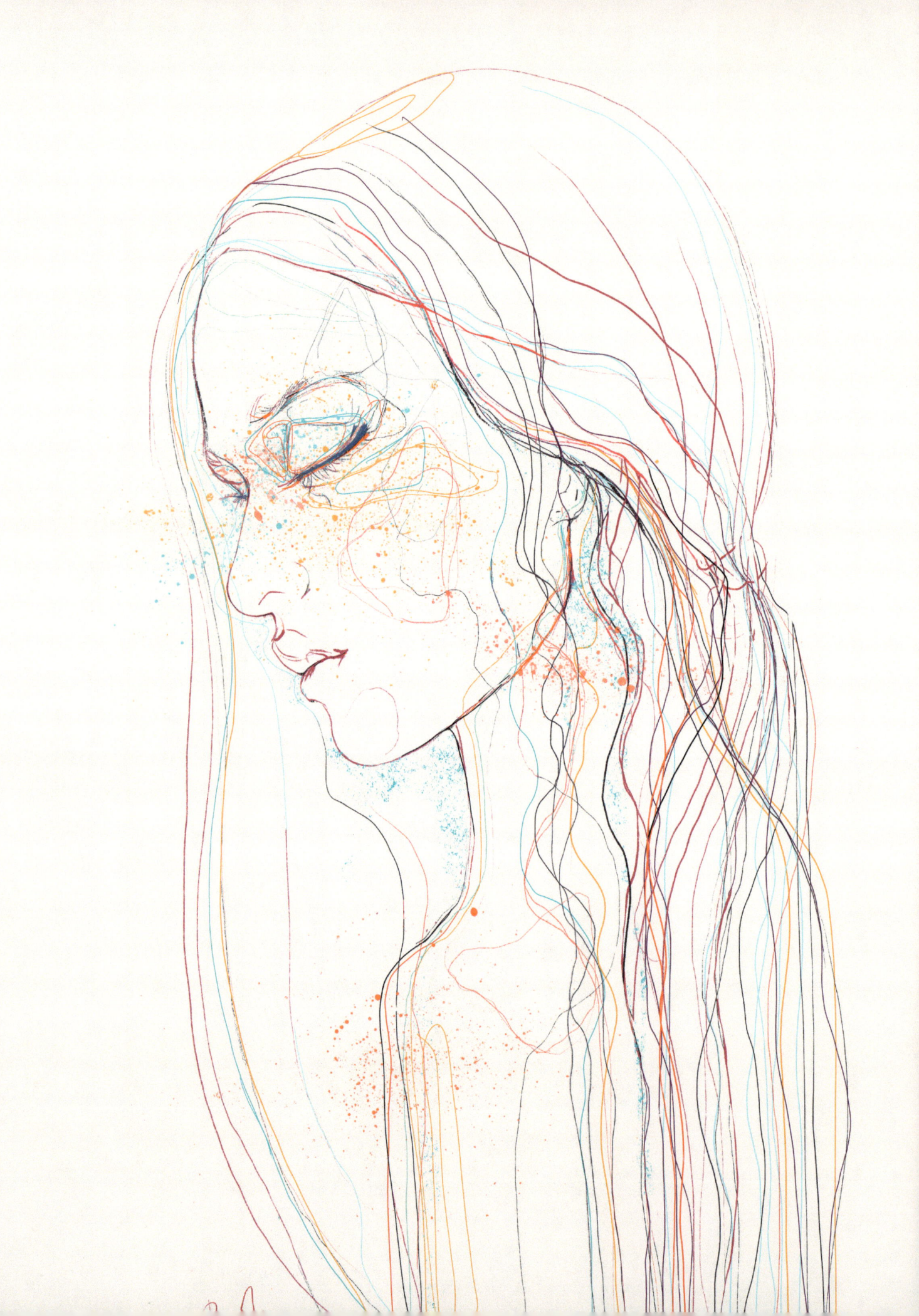

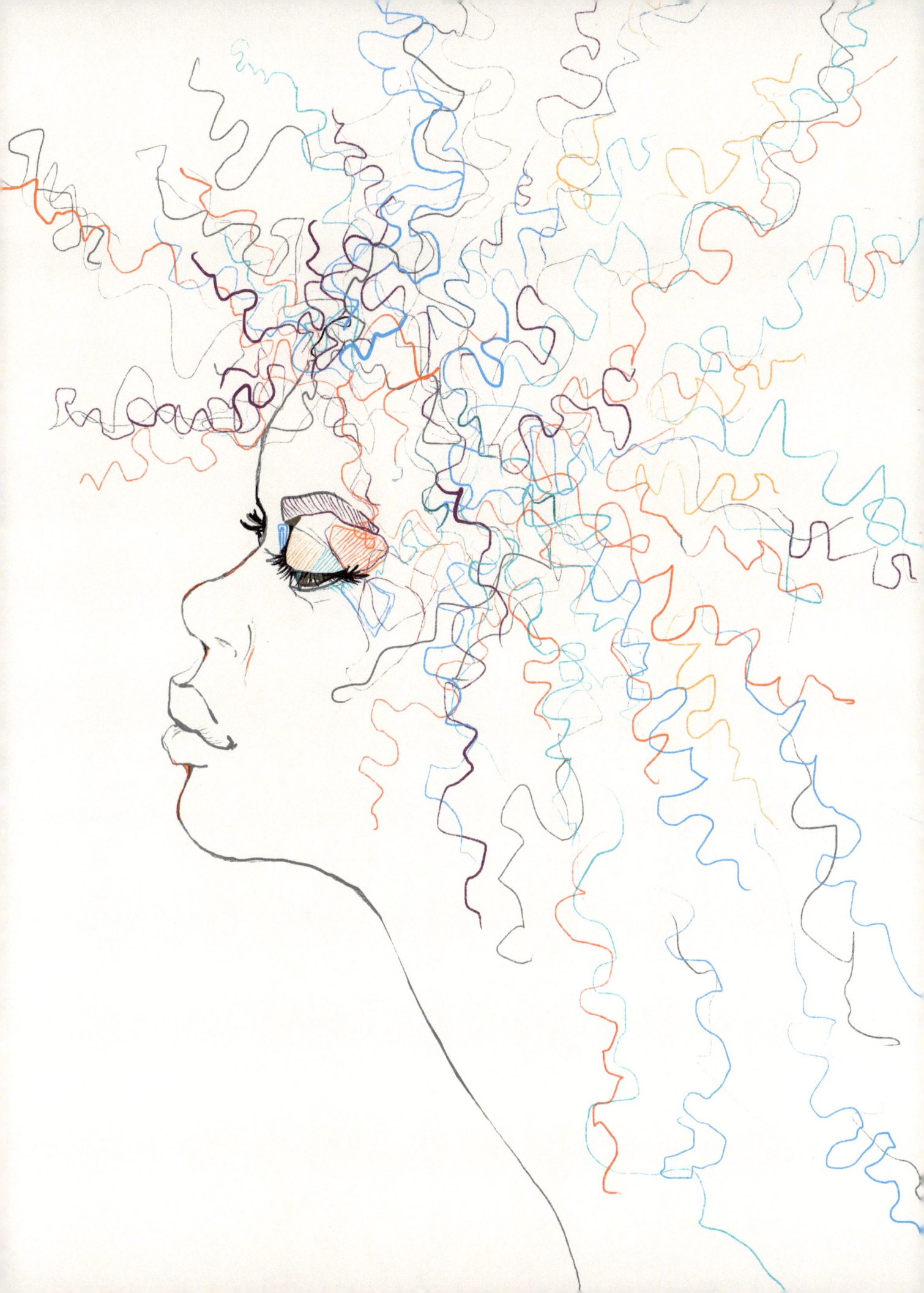

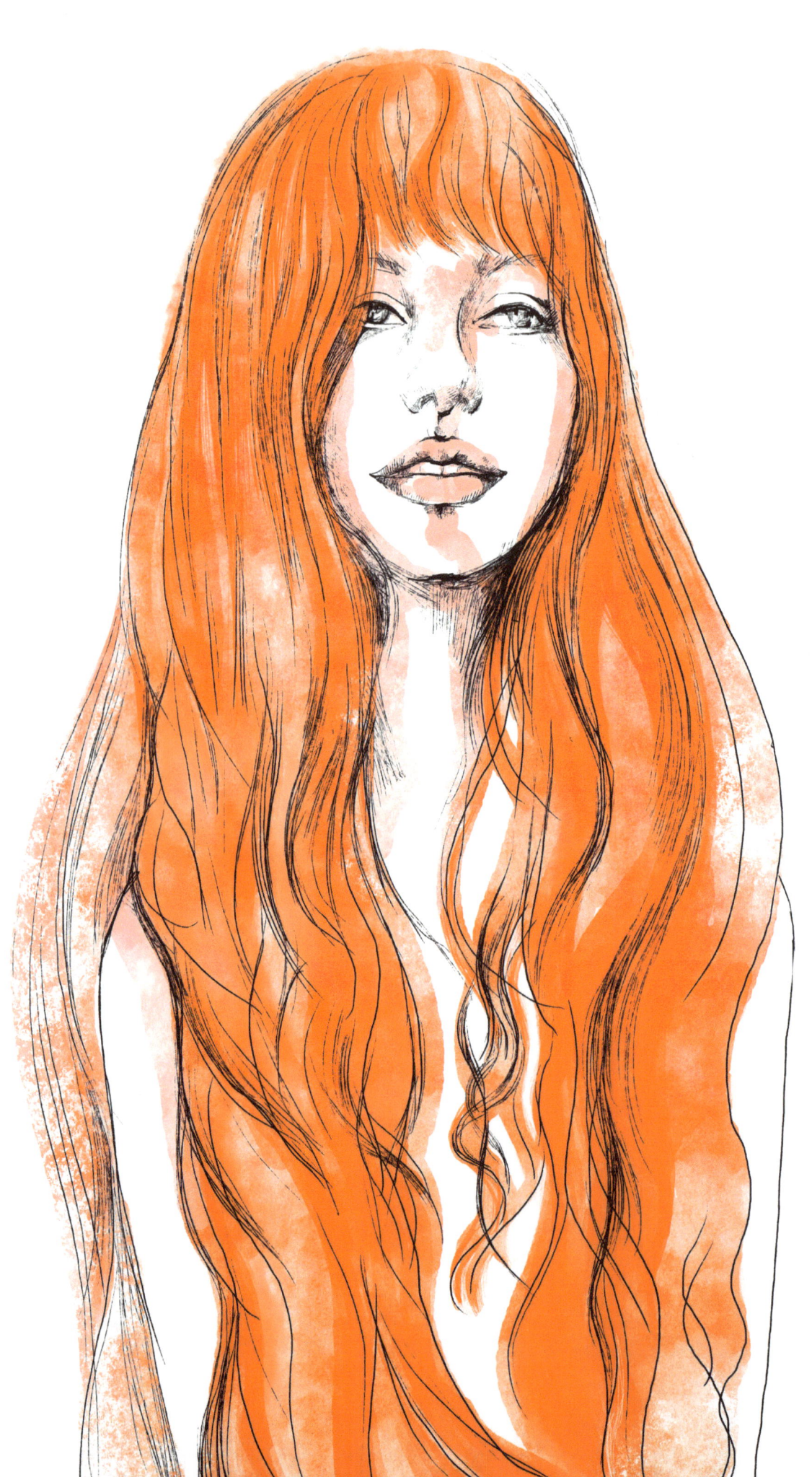

The Ginger Look

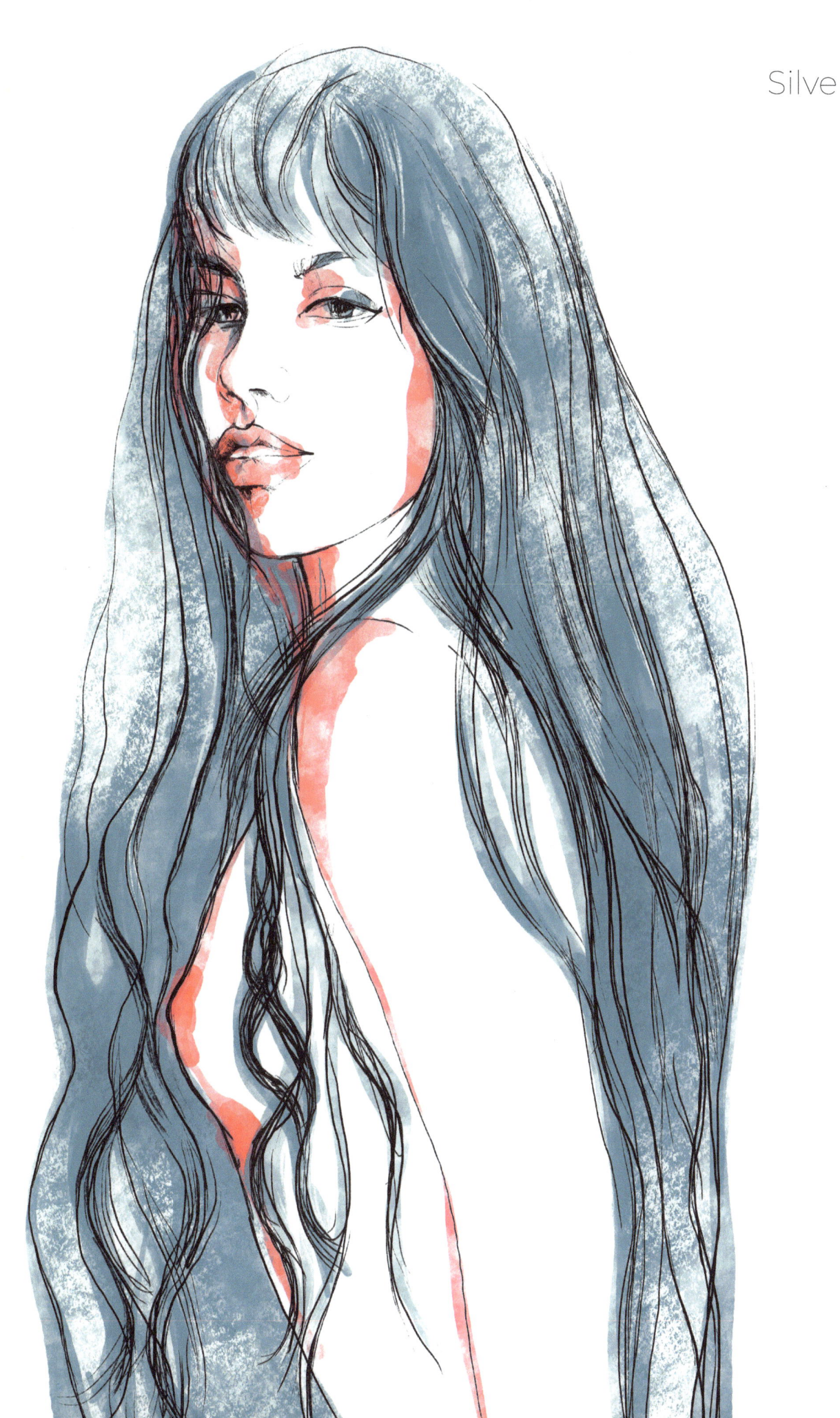

Silver

# BEAUTIFUL PORTRAITS of everyday people

## The Portrait Commissions

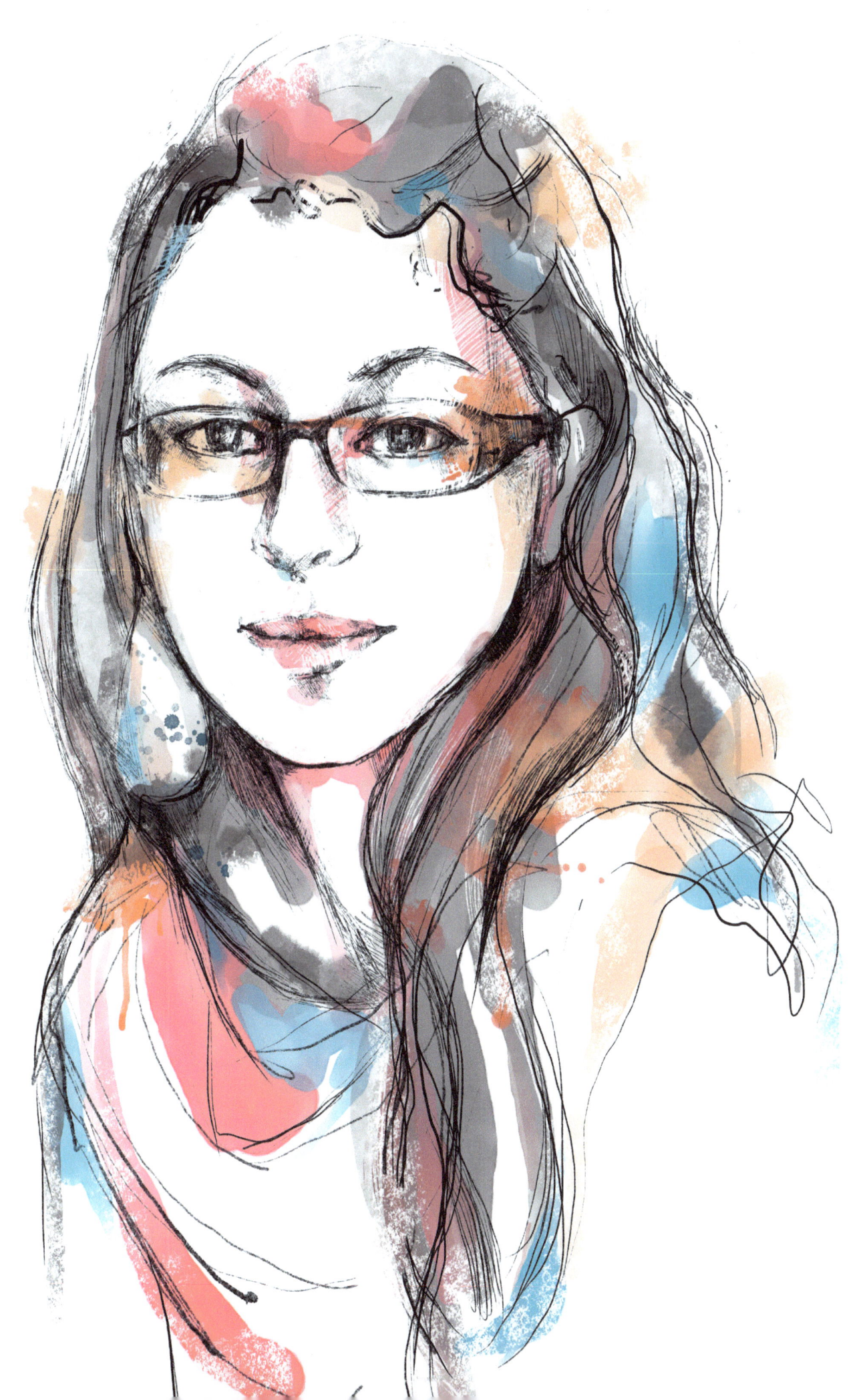

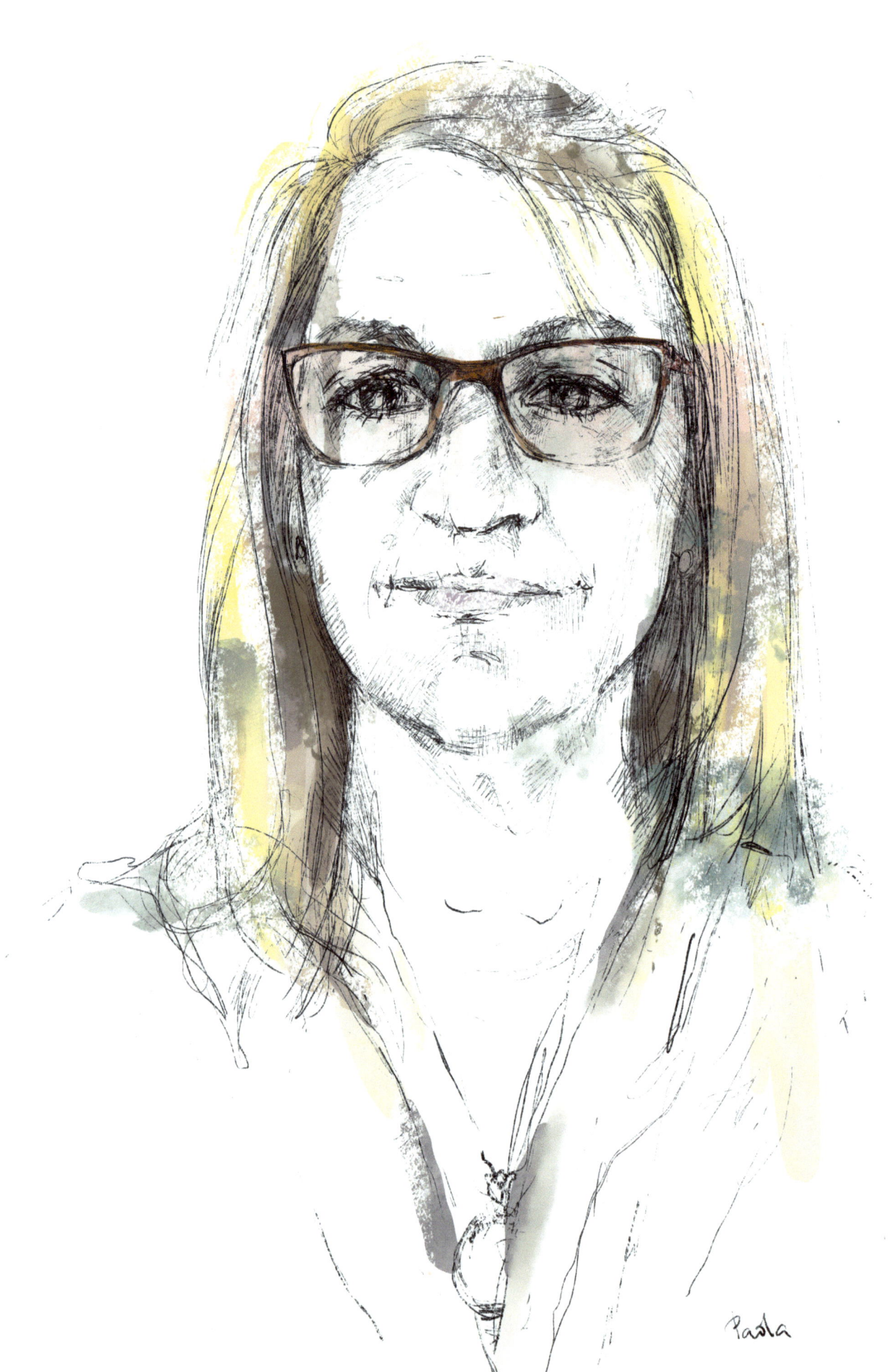

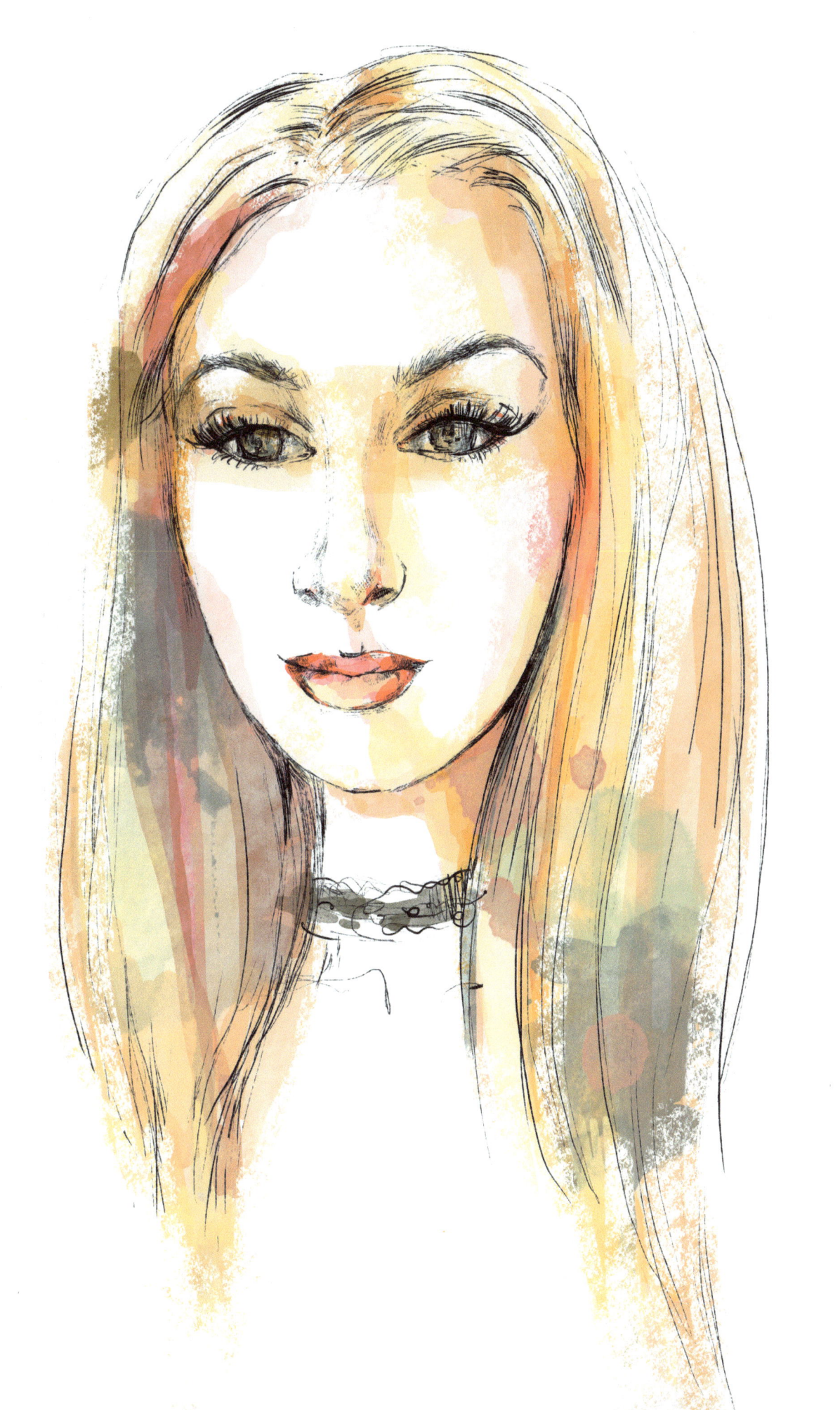

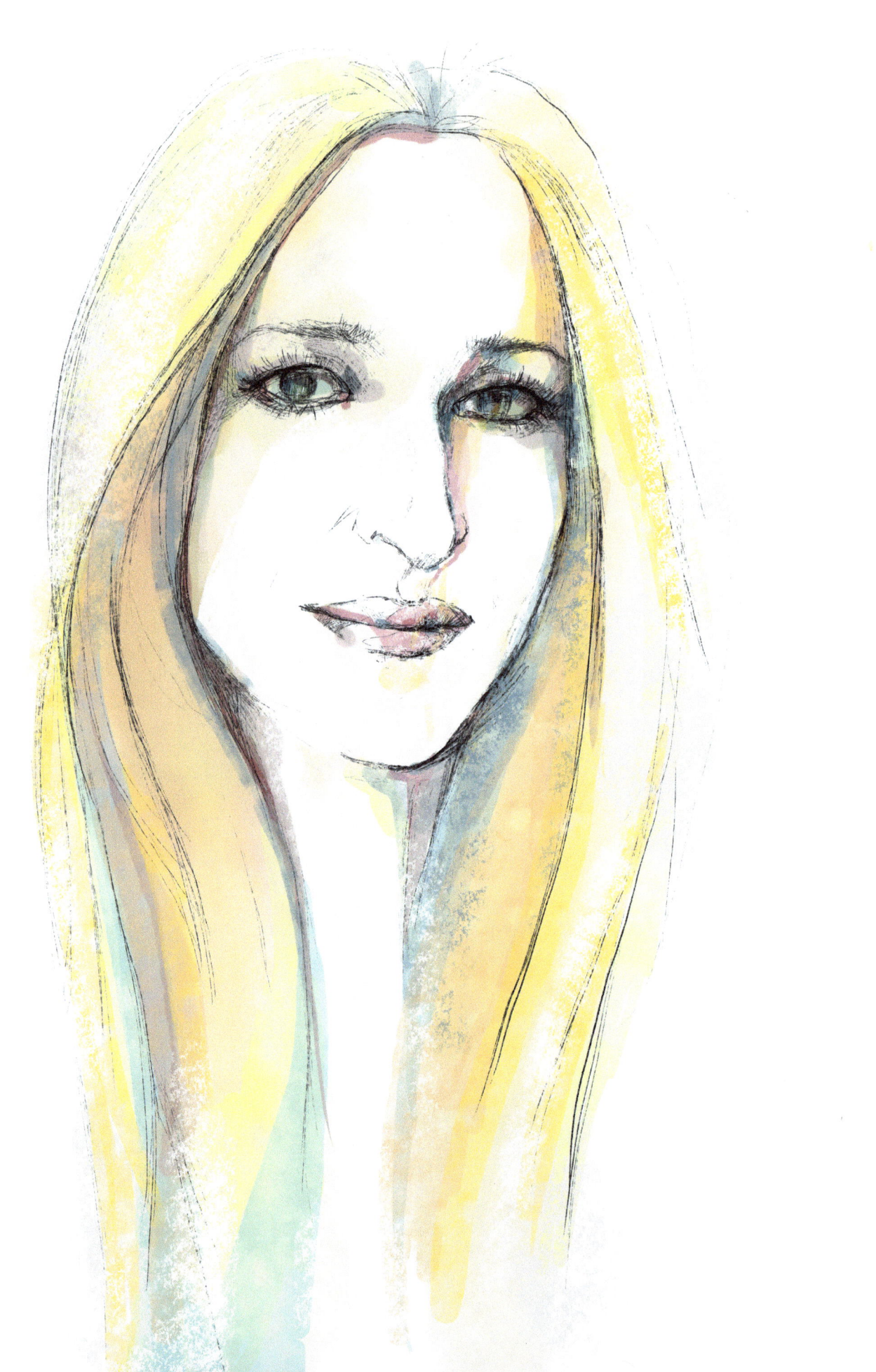

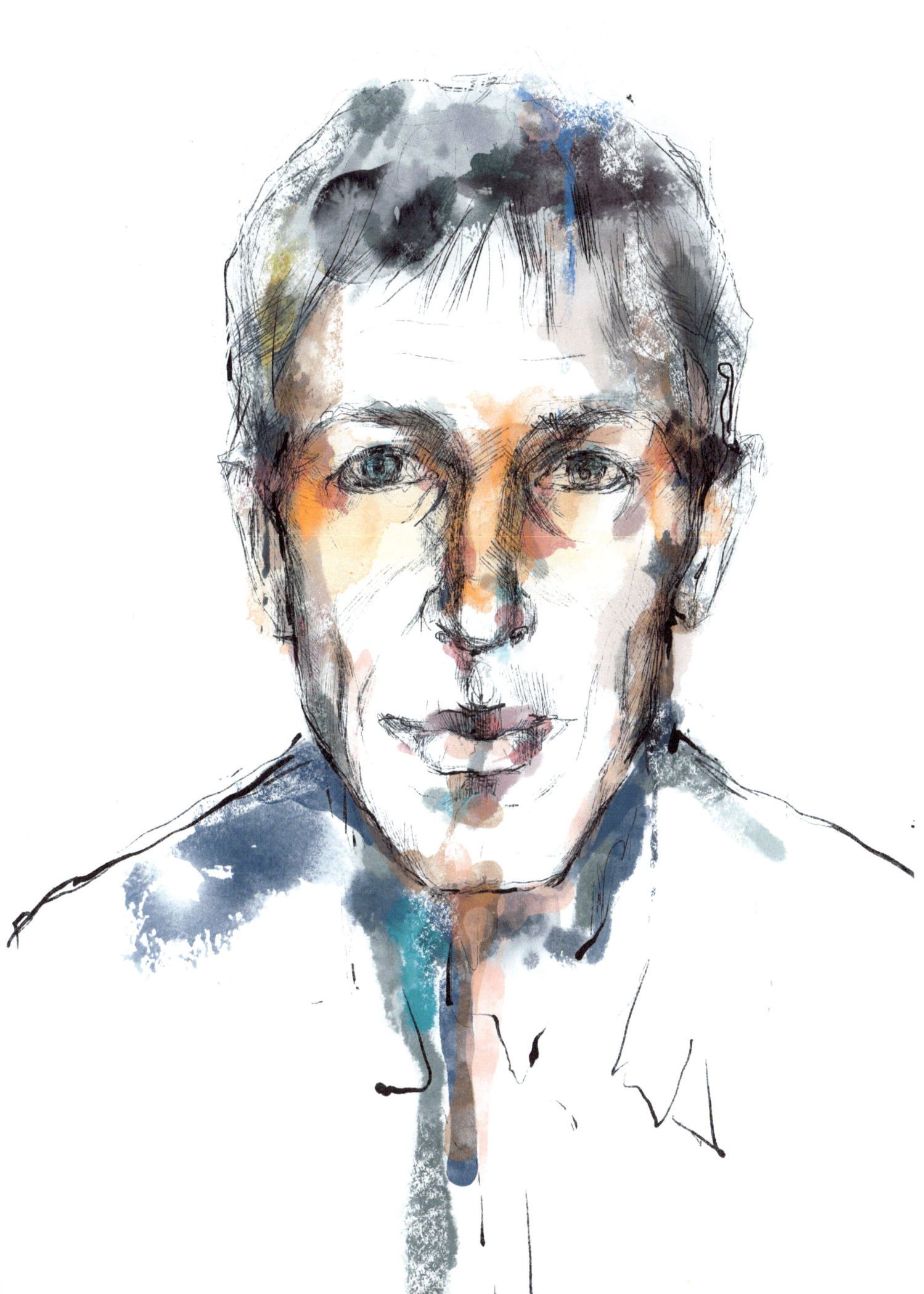

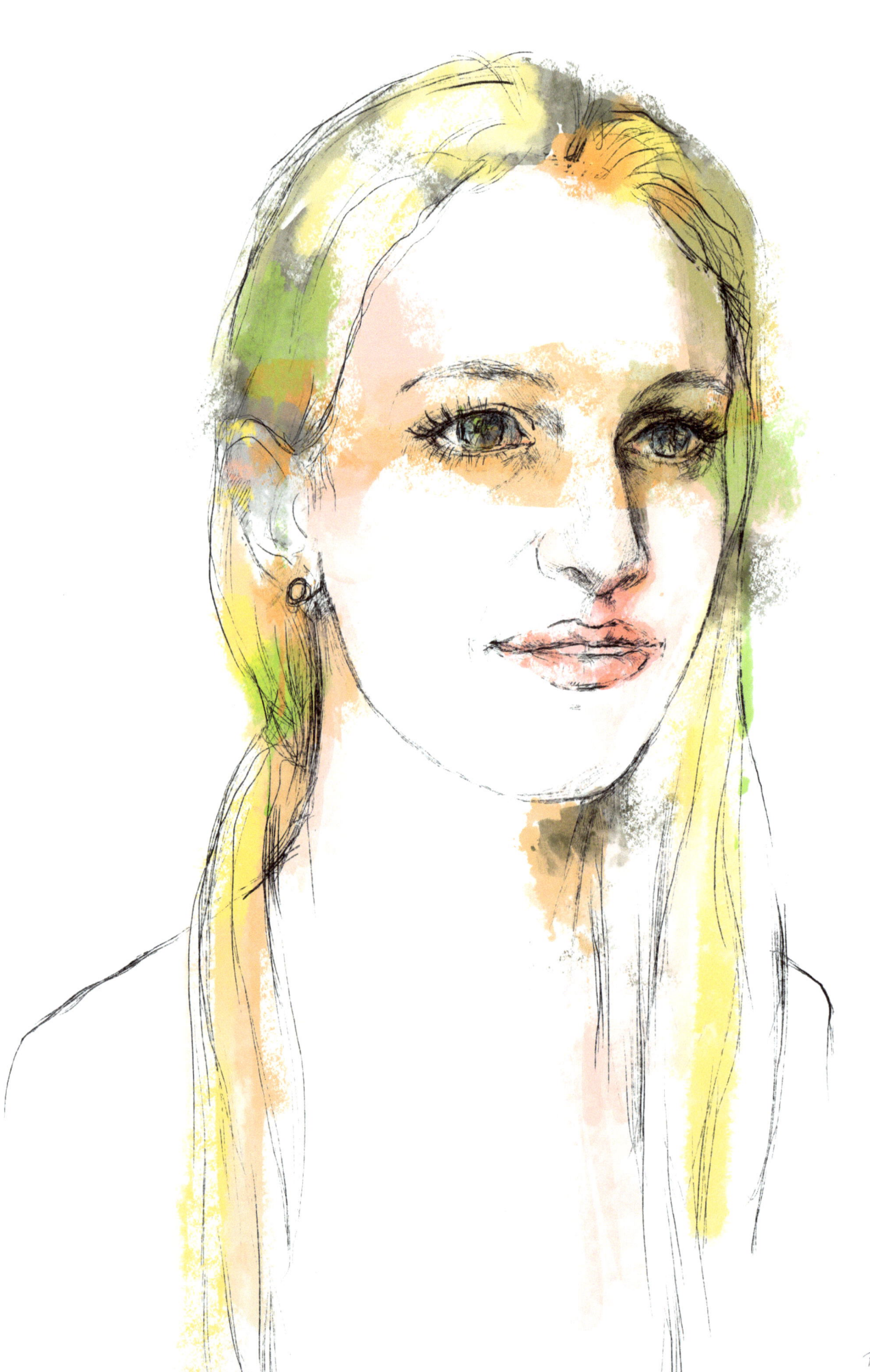

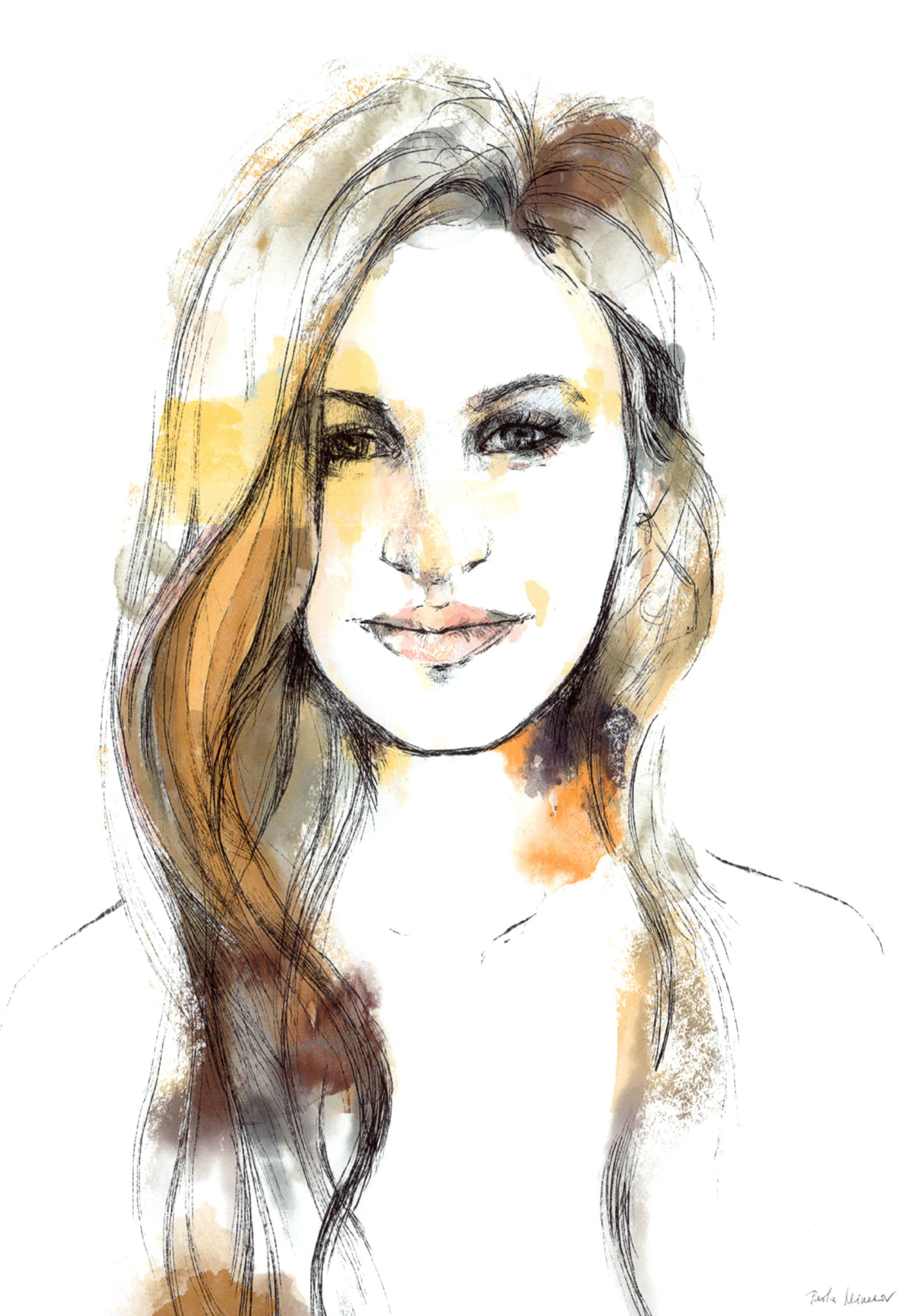

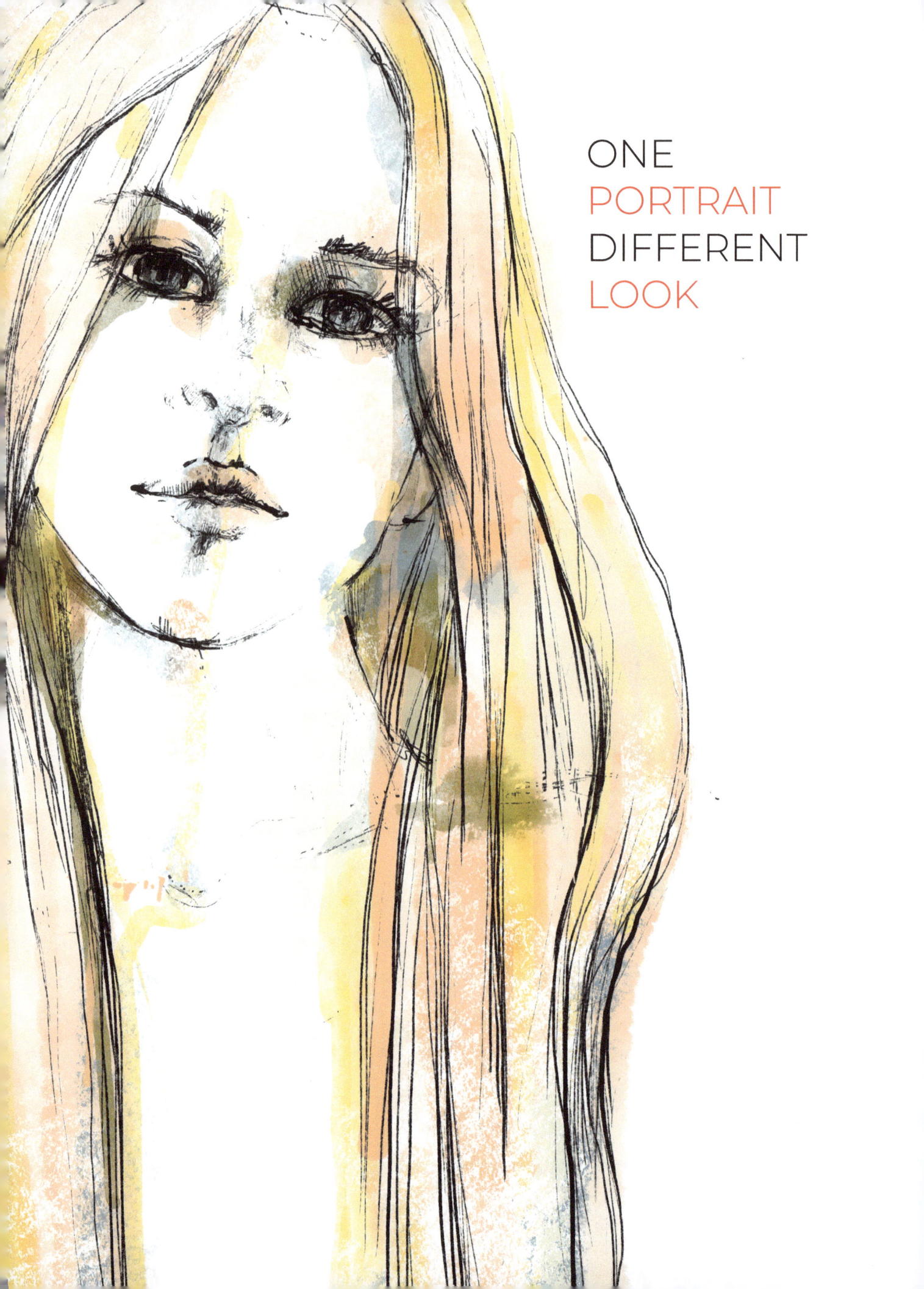

ONE PORTRAIT
DIFFERENT LOOK

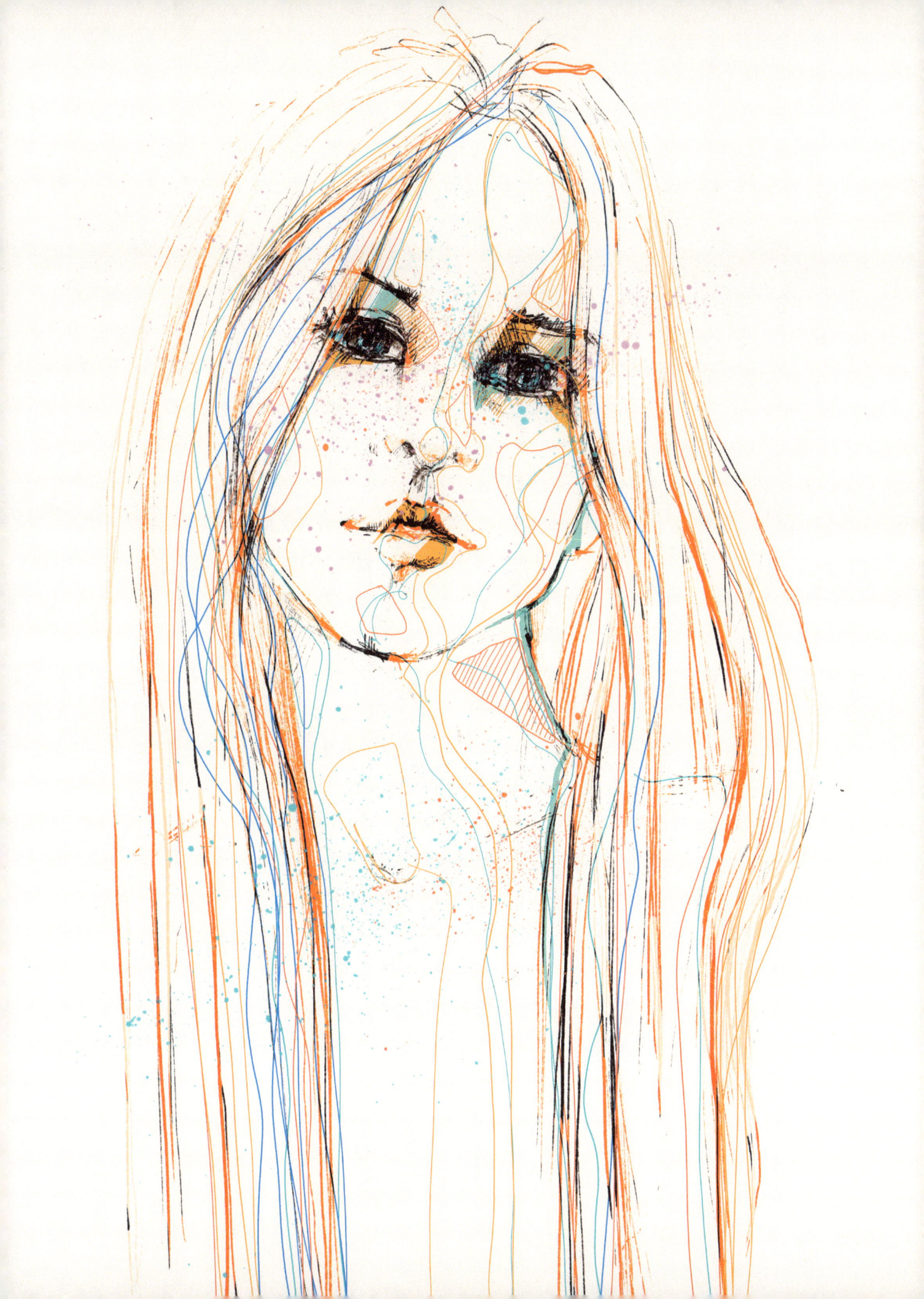

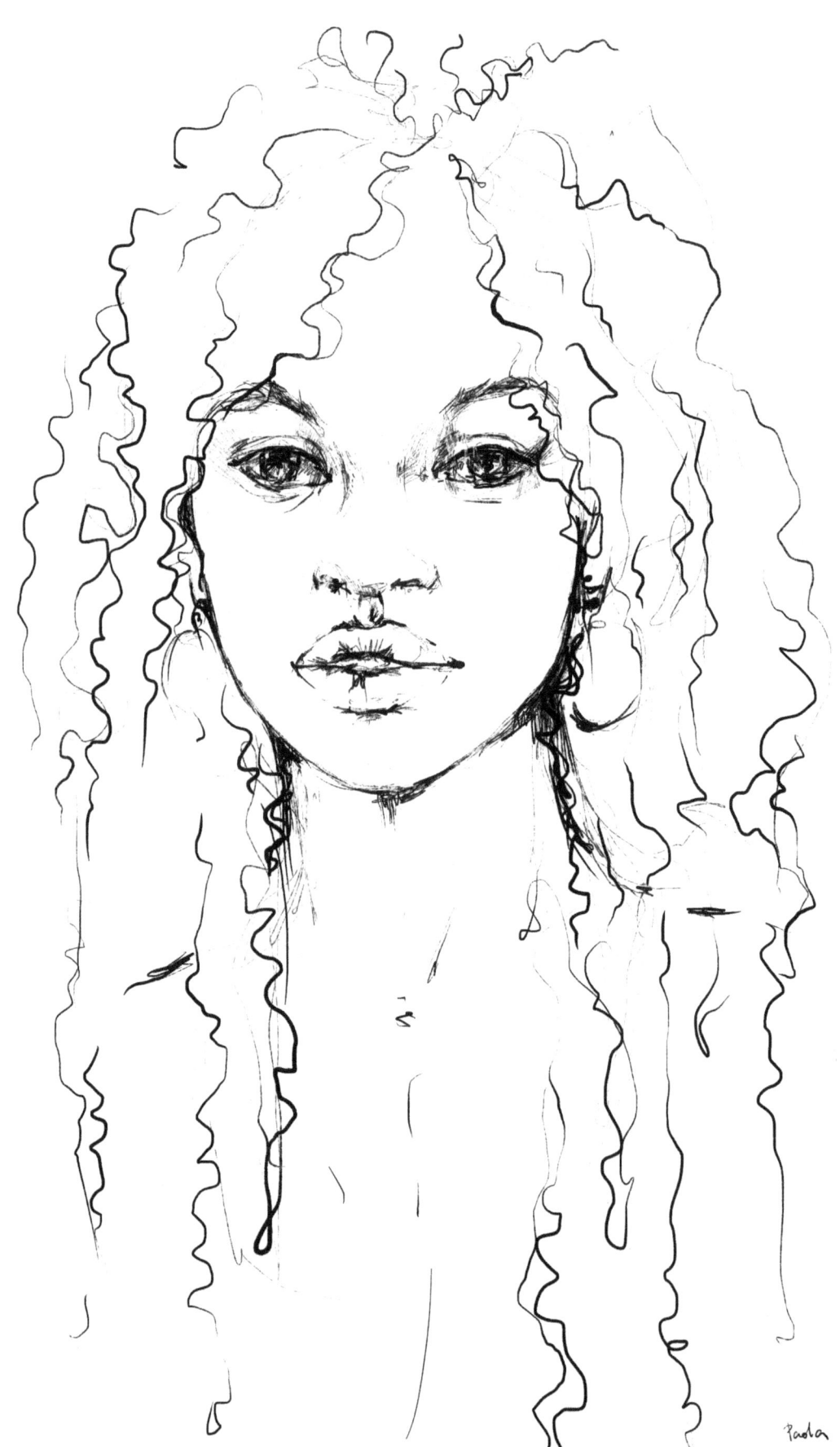

Violet

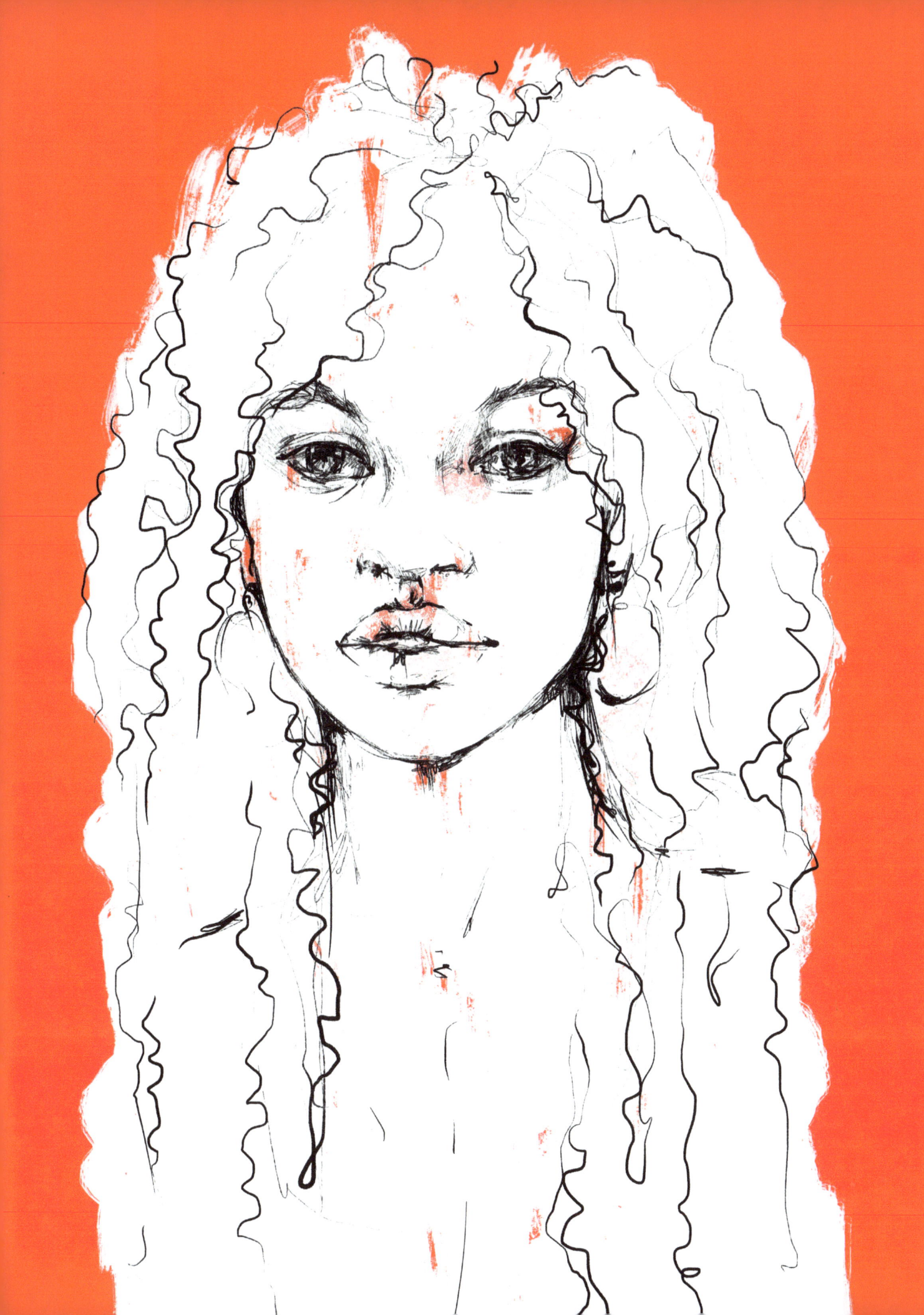

Couple's Portraits

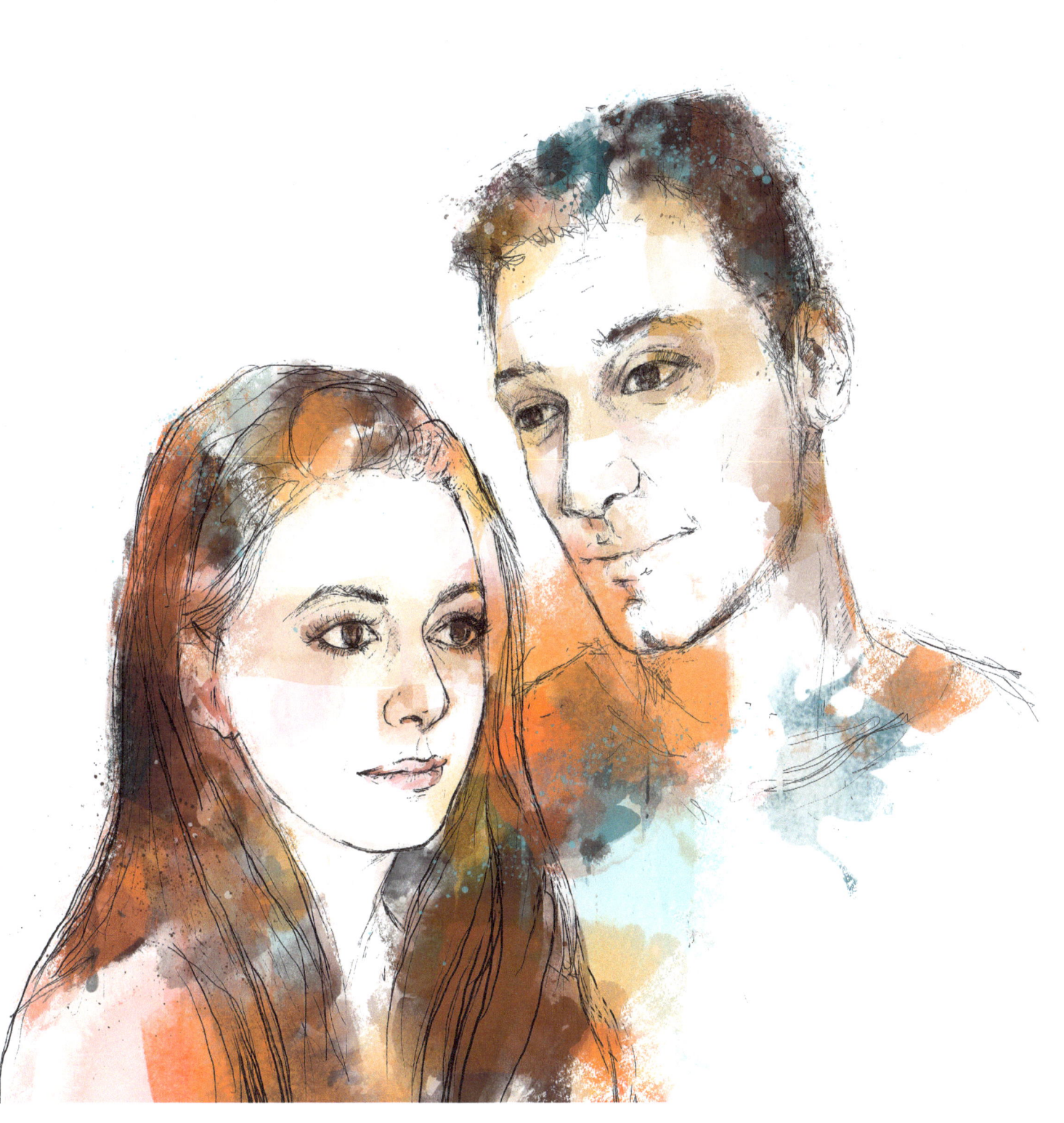

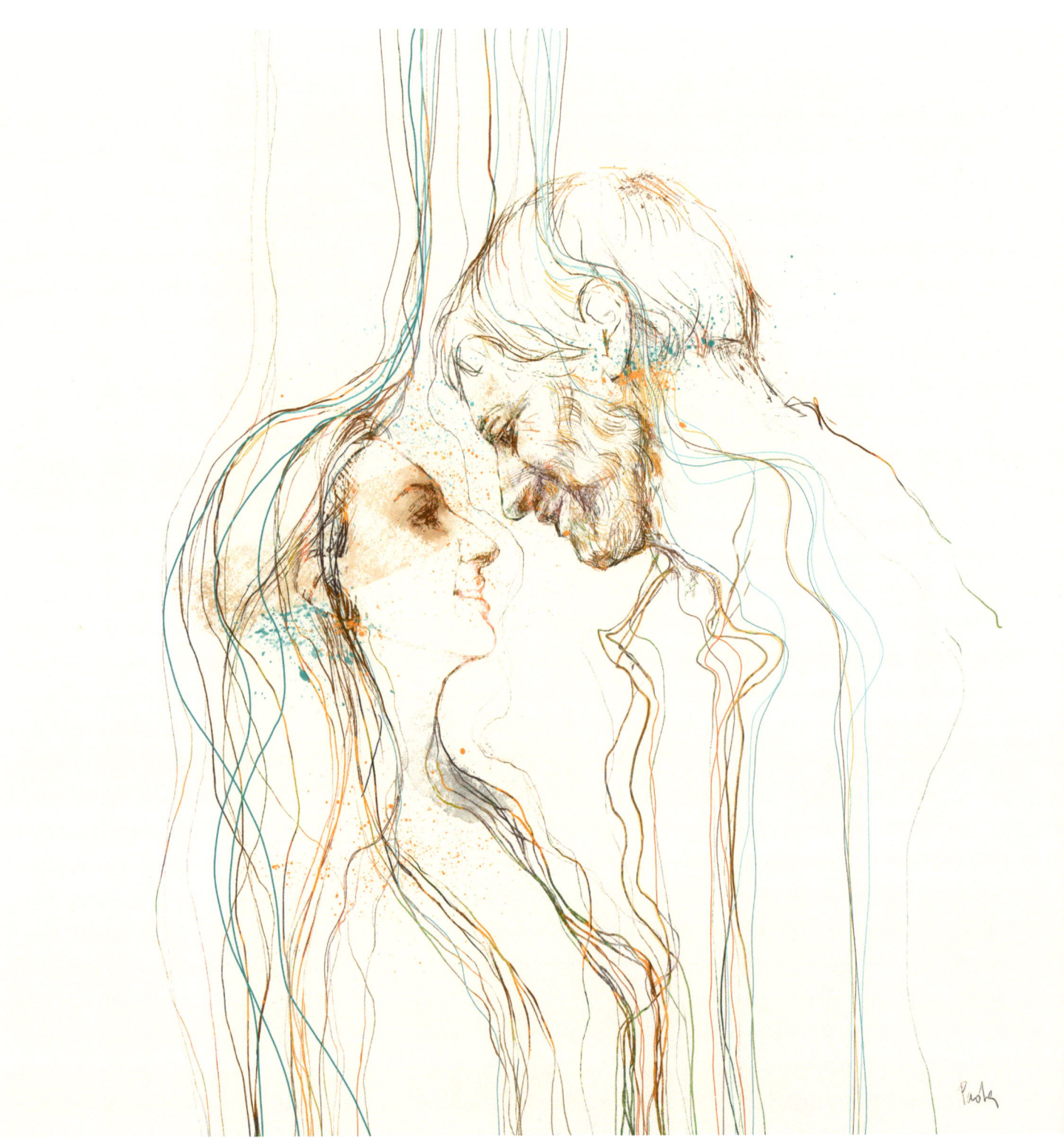

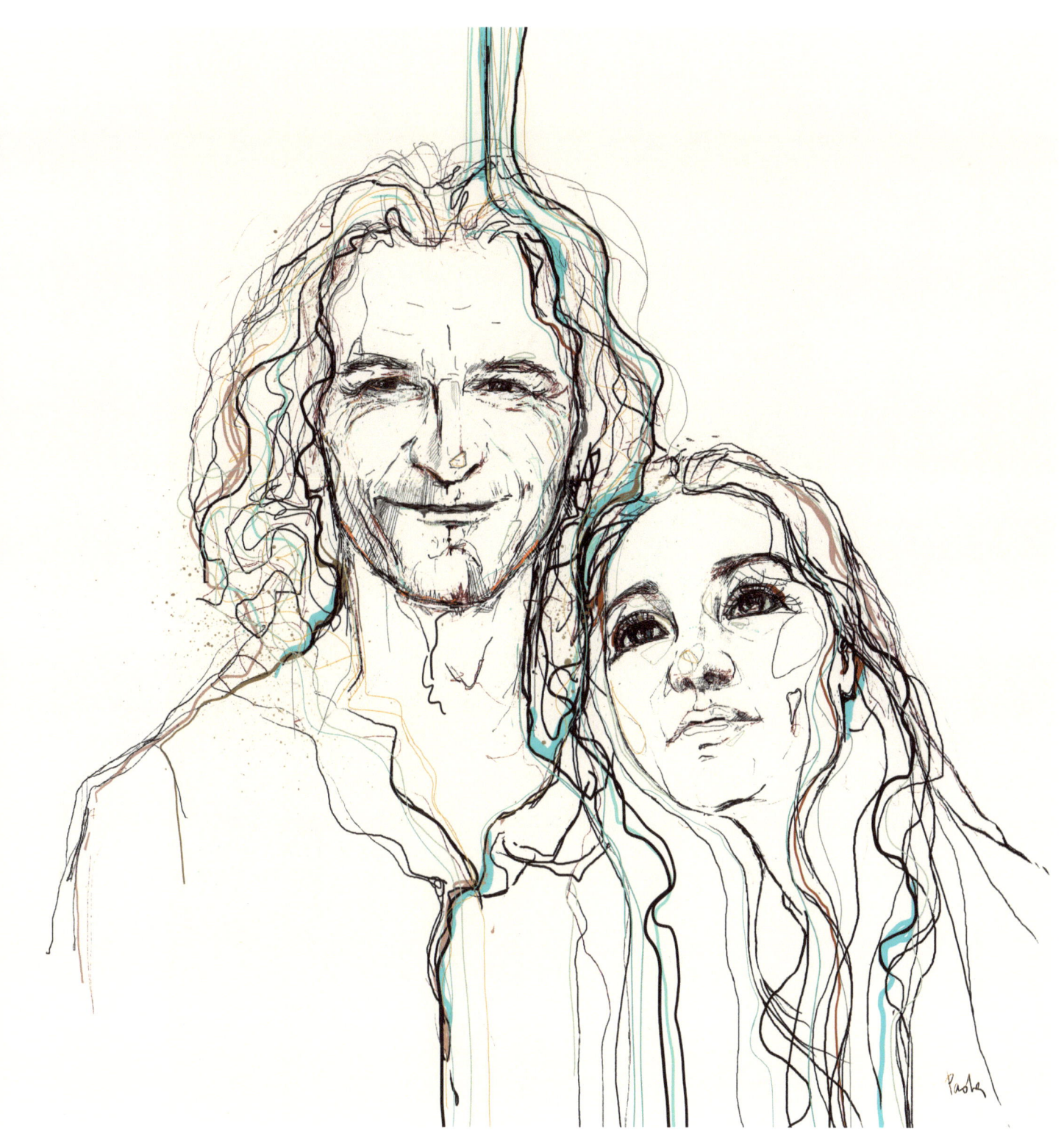

# Portraits of Children

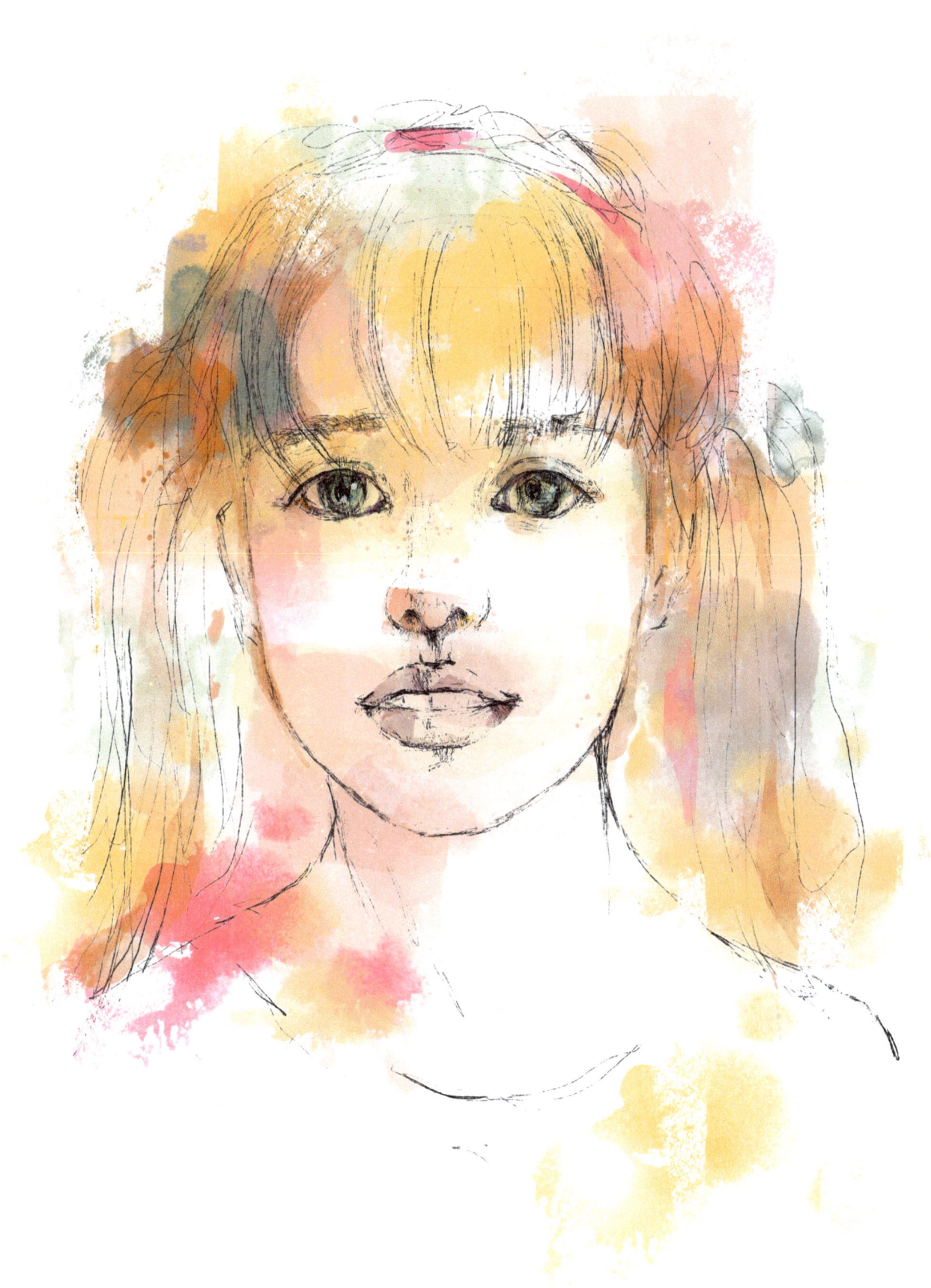

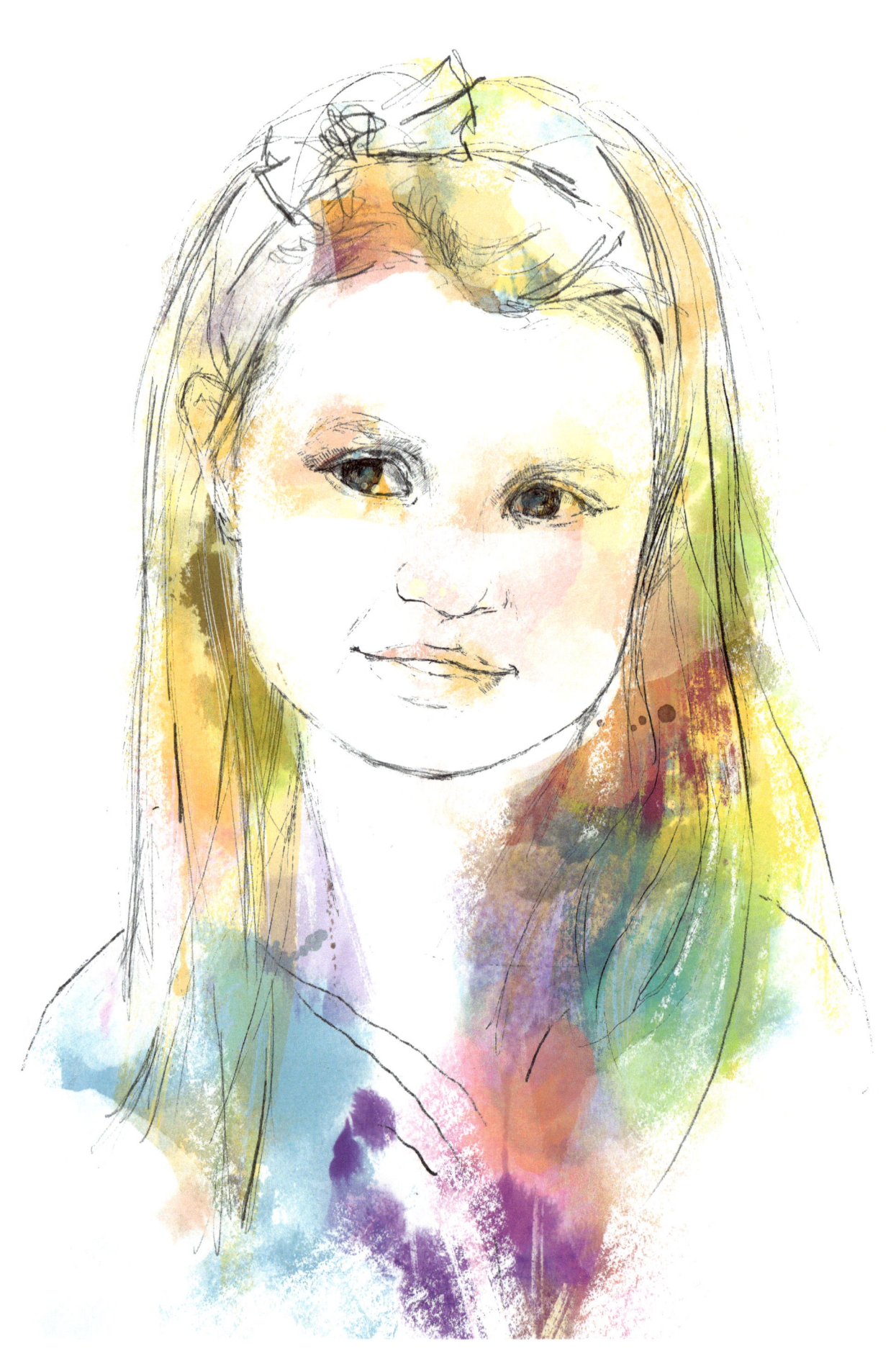

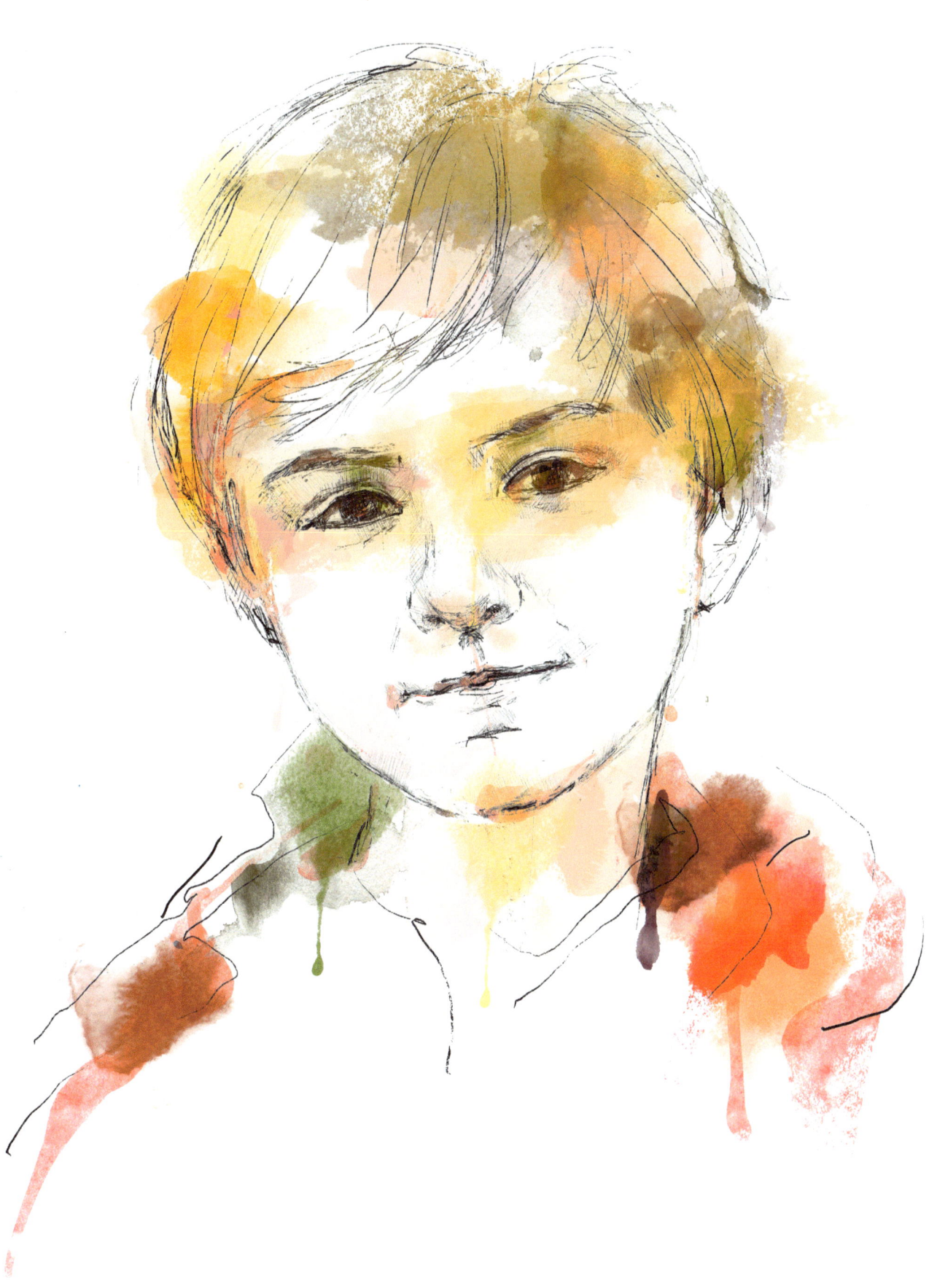

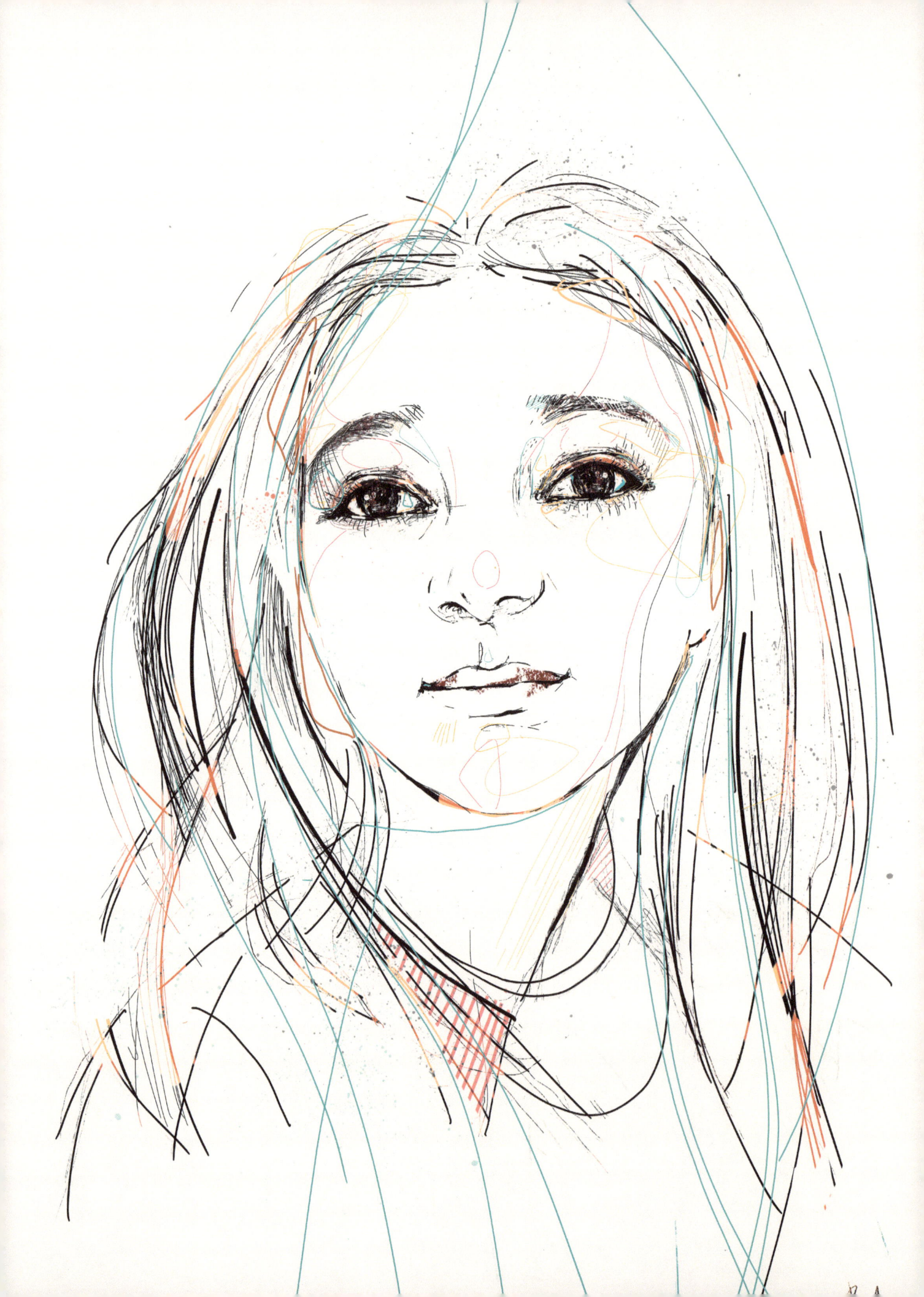

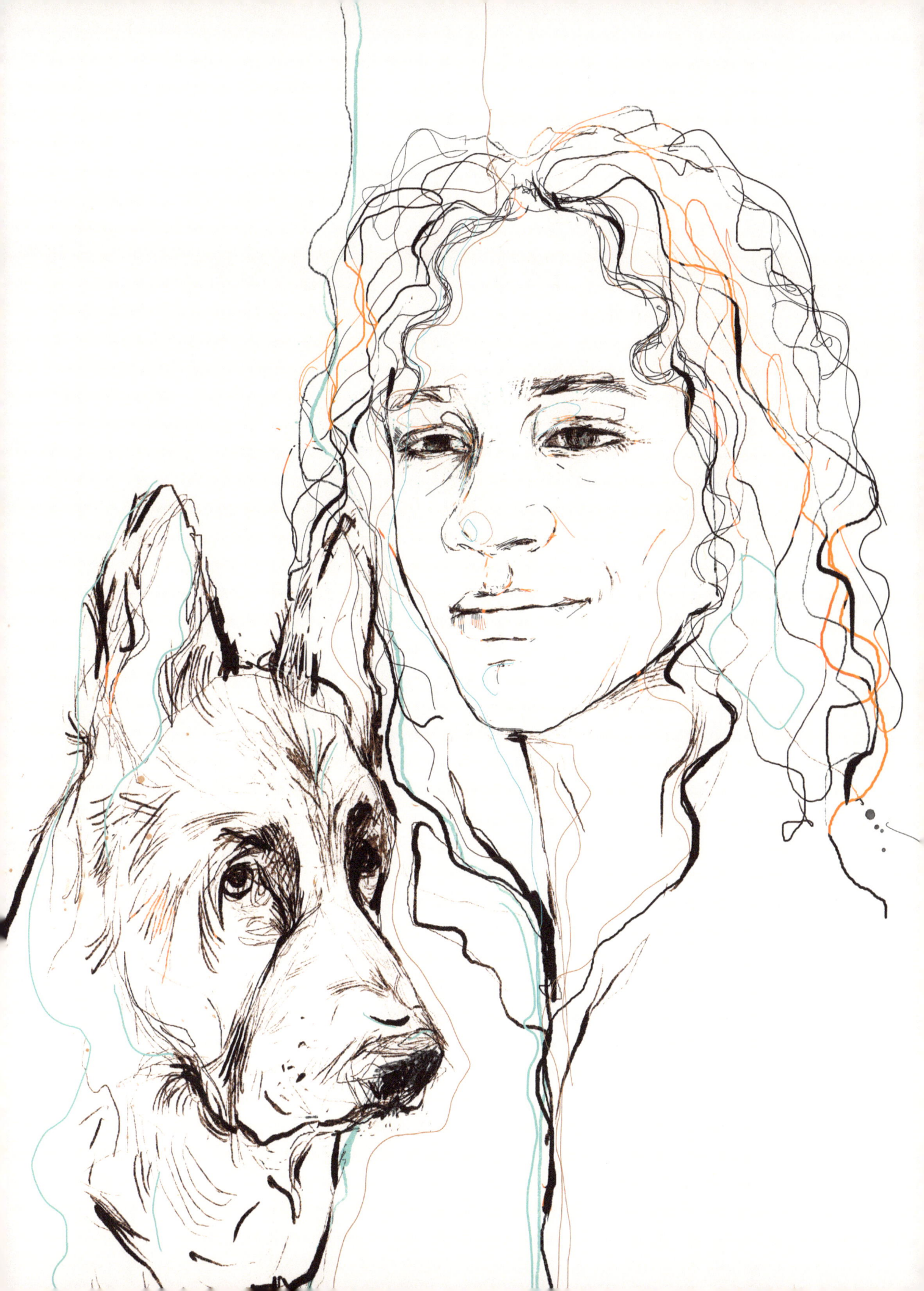

**HOME** is not a place, it's a **FEELING**

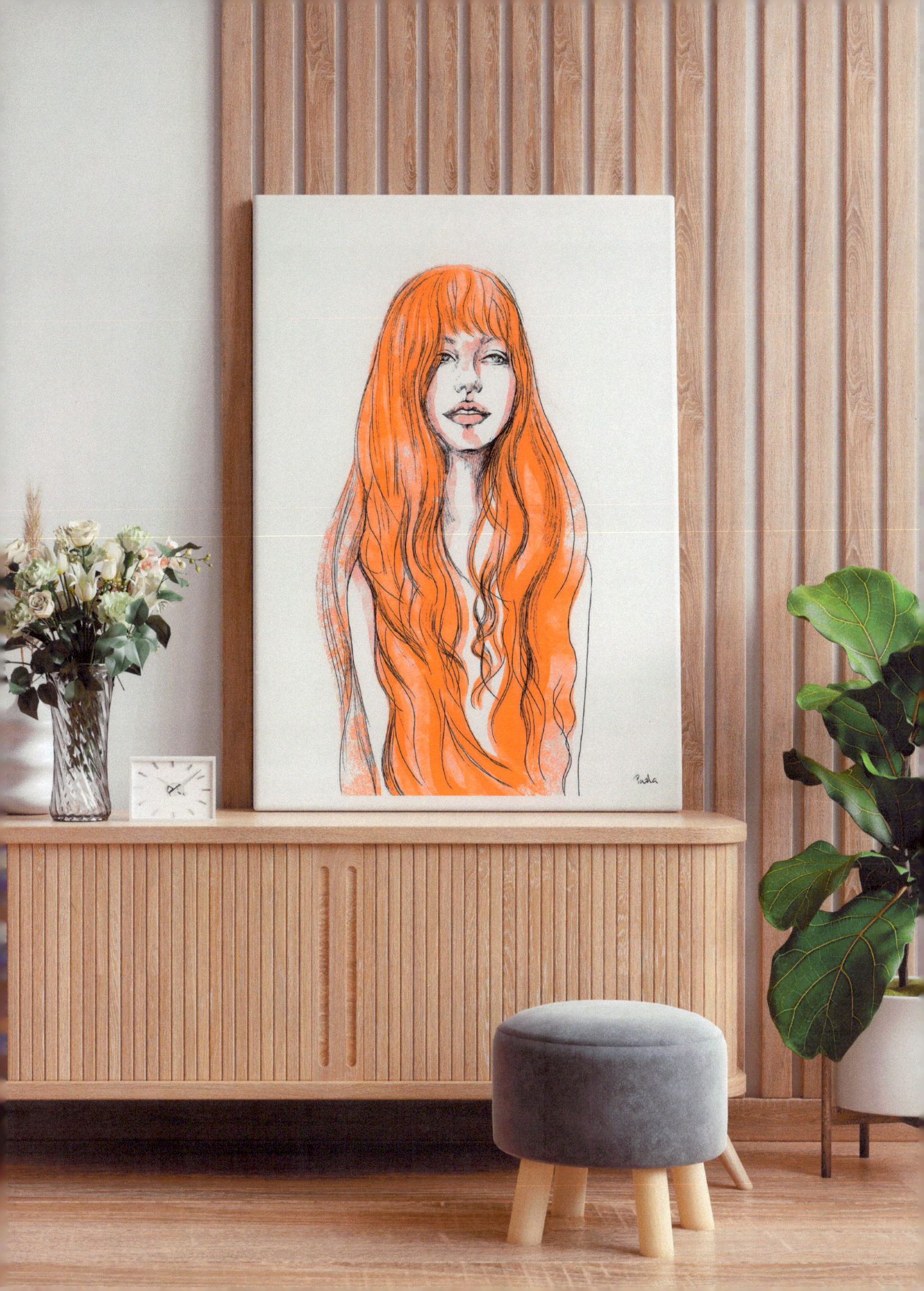

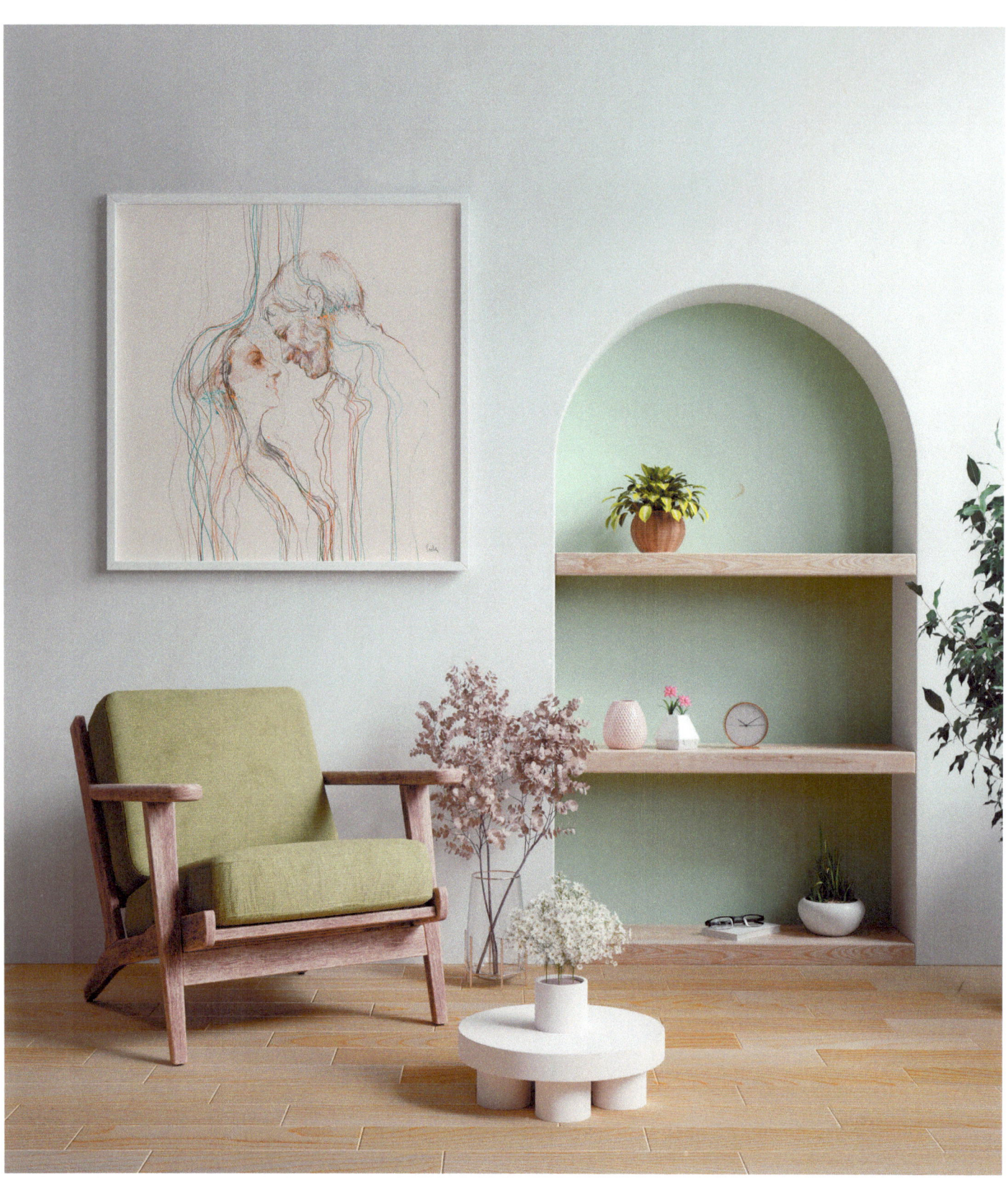

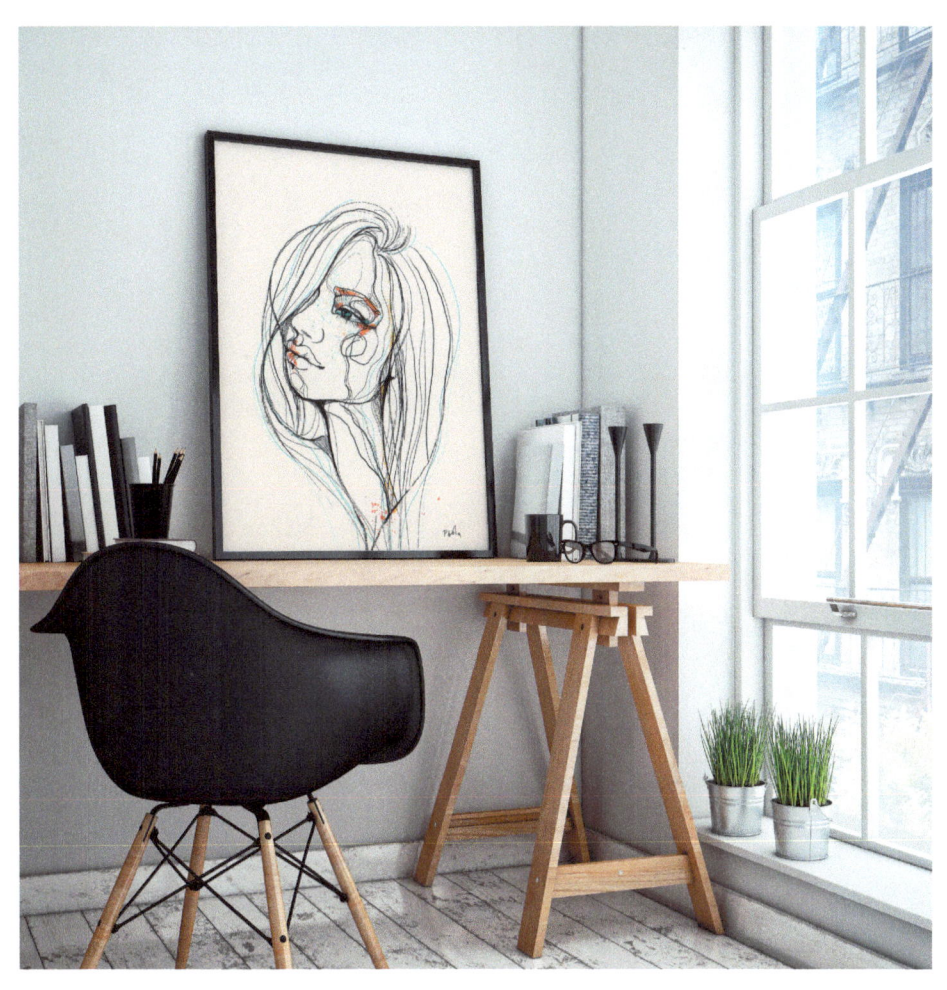
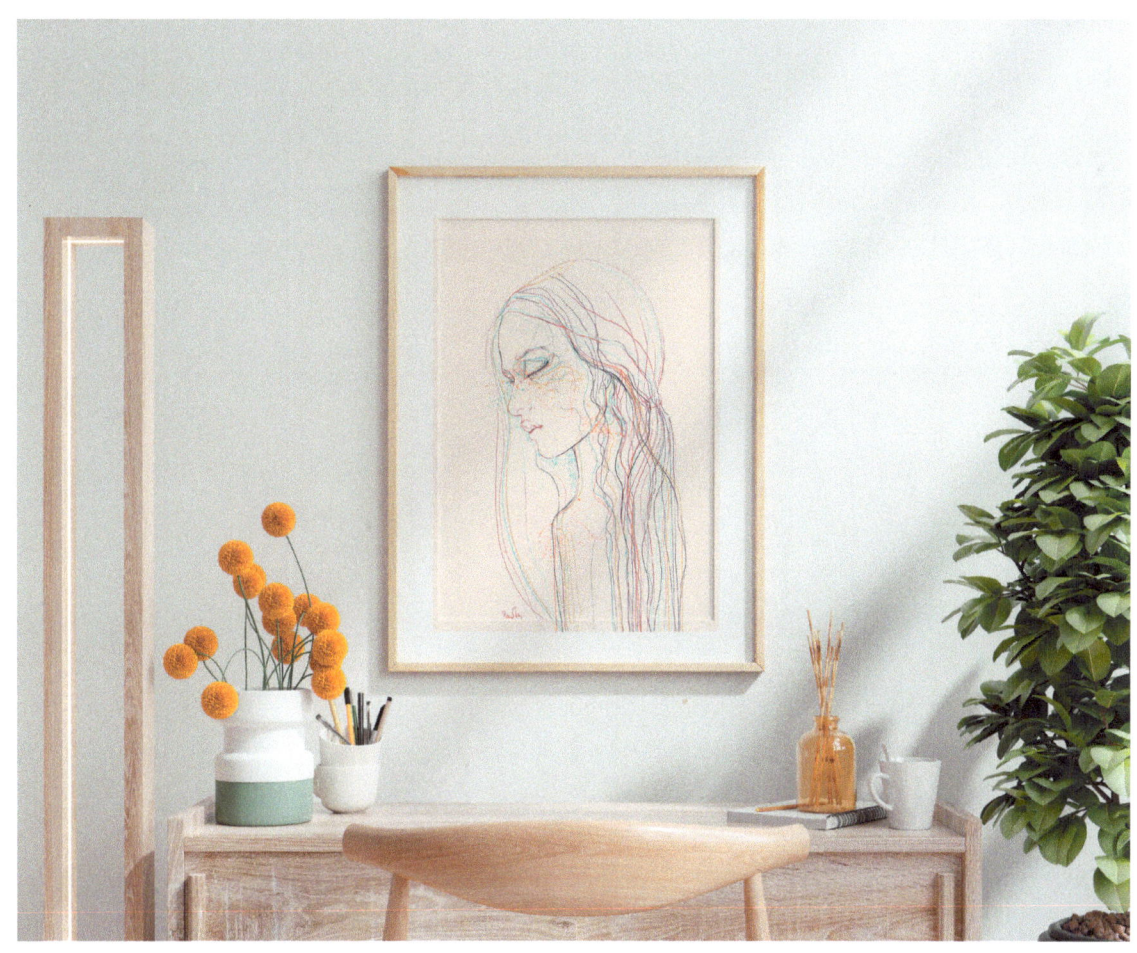

# CONTACT

email: studio@paola.art
website: https://paola.art

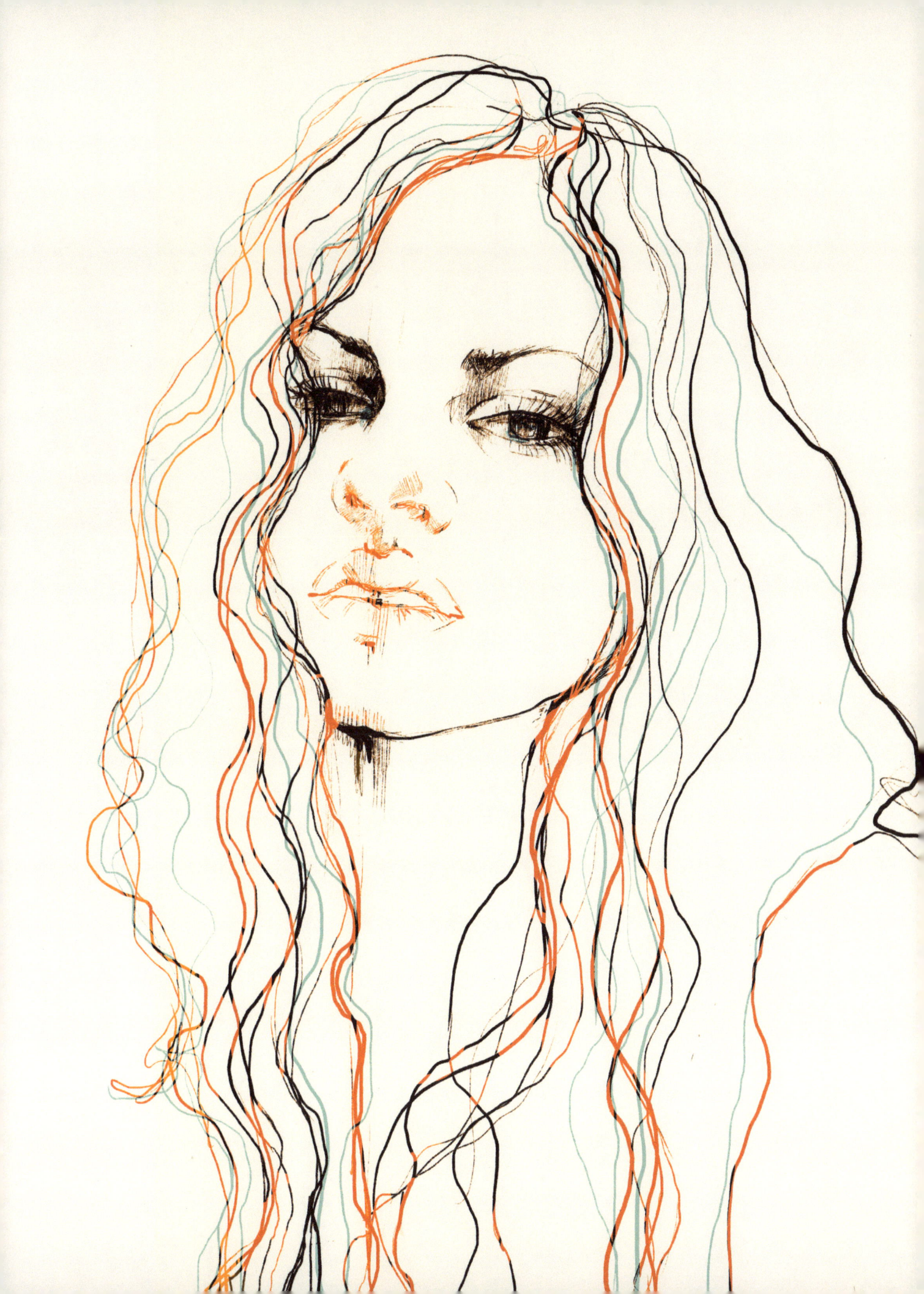